Spies and Spying

CODES AND CODEBREAKING

Andrew Langley

Smart Apple Media

Smart Apple Media
P.O. Box 3263
Mankato, MN 56002

Printed in the United States of America

Library of Congress Cataloging-in-Publication Data

Langley, Andrew.
  Codes and codebreaking / Andrew Langley.
     p. cm. -- (Spies and spying)
  Includes index.
  ISBN 978-1-59920-357-7
  1. Cryptography--History--Juvenile literature. 2. Ciphers--History--Juvenile literature. I. Title.
  Z103.3.L36 2010
  652'.8--dc22

                                                                          2008055503

Created by Q2AMedia
Editor: Jean Coppendale
Art Director: Rahul Dhiman
Designer: Ranjan Singh
Picture Researcher: Shreya Sharma
Line Artist: Sibi N. Devasia
Coloring Artist: Mahender Kumar

All words in **bold** can be found in the glossary on pages 30–31.

Web site information is correct at time of going to press. However, the publishers cannot
accept liability for any information or links found on third-party web sites.

Picture credits
t=top b=bottom c=center l=left r=right
Cover Images: Shutterstock, Inset: Q2AMedia: t, Tim Jenner/ Shutterstock: c, Q2AMedia: b.

Insides: Tim Jenner/ Shutterstock: Title Page, Maxim Kulko/ Shutterstock: 4bl, Adistock/ Shutterstock: 4br, Bettmann/ Corbis: 5,
Itechno/ Dreamstime: 7tl, The National Archives: 11bl, Brandon Seidel/ Shutterstock: 11cr, Archie Miles/ Alamy: 12, Hulton-Deutsch
Collection/ Corbis: 13cr, Tim Jenner/ Shutterstock: 13t, Adrio Communications Ltd/ Shutterstock: 14, The Natinal Archive: 16, Helge
Fykse Norway/ Af.Mil: 18, The National Security Agency/ Central Security Service: 19c, Ian Miles-Flashpoint Pictures / Alamy: 19b,
Time & Life Pictures/ Getty Images: 19tr, The National Security Agency/ Central Security Service: 20, Associated Press: 21, Samuel
Tom Holiday: 22br,Corbis: 23, The National Archive: 24, The National Security Agency/ Central Security Service: 24, Spectral/ 123RF:
26t, Ilker Canikligil/ Shutterstock: 26b, Tony Medici/ USA Army: 27b, Ilker Canikligil/ Shutterstock: 28, Mikael Karlsson / Alamy: 29,
Tim Jenner/ Shutterstock: 31.

Q2AMedia Art Bank: Title Page, 6, 7bl, 8tl, 8br, 9tr, 9b, 10cr, 10br, 15, 17t, 17b, 27tr, 29tr.

9 8 7 6 5 4 3 2 1

CONTENTS

SENDING SECRETS

One of the most important things a spy does is find out secrets. This information then has to be sent back to base in secret! To do this, spies send coded messages.

In Disguise

Many types of messages are sent by spies. During a war, messages may contain details of an attack, or plans for a new weapon. In peacetime, it could be information about a **mole** planted in the enemy camp. Important information can be disguised by putting it in code. A coded message can look like nonsense—a string of numbers or meaningless words. Only someone who knows how the code works is able to understand it.

There are many ways to disguise messages. Some use pictures instead of words, and others use number sequences.

Codes and Ciphers

Throughout history hundreds of different codes have been developed. Some use letters, numbers, or symbols in place of words. These are called **ciphers**. However, as soon as a code is invented, someone will try to break it. A very simple cipher might replace "A" with "1," "B" with "2," "C" with "3," and so on. This would not take long to break. Other methods of hiding words are much more complicated.

This U.S. Marine sergeant is using a **cryptograph**. This was a device used to **decode** secret messages during World War II. Many women were involved in the science of cryptography during the war and dealt with encoding and decoding important messages.

Top Secret

The simplest way of hiding a message is to write it in invisible ink.

1. Write the message on paper in lemon juice (which has no color).
2. Send the invisible message.
3. To read it, gently heat the paper. The writing will become visible.

ANCIENT SECRETS

The earliest kinds of codes were just ways of hiding a message so that the enemy could not see it—let alone read it.

Headlines

Around 500 B.C., Histiaeus of Miletus wanted to send a secret message to another Greek leader, asking him to go to war against the Persians. But Persian soldiers watched all the roads. So Histiaeus shaved the head of his most loyal slave and tattooed the words on it. When the slave's hair had grown long again, he set off to deliver the message. At his destination, the slave had his head shaved so the message could be read.

The Ancient Greeks and Persians used spies to find out the location of each other's armies. Each wanted to have an advantage over the other before they met on the battlefield.

Julius Caesar (100–44 B.C.)

The Roman general and leader invented a code which is named after him—the Caesar Cipher. It replaced letters with the ones which came three places after them in the normal alphabet. In this code, the name CAESAR becomes FDHVDU.

SPY FILE

Making Codes More Complicated

A tattoo was a simple way of hiding a message but it did not hide the meaning. If a Persian had shaved the messenger's head, he would have understood the message. So codemakers developed ways to hide the meaning of words by changing the letters. This could be done in two ways—by moving the letters into a different order, or by replacing each letter with another one, according to a set pattern.

Top Secret

The Spartan code stick

The Spartans of Ancient Greece developed a simple code in about 450 B.C. They disguised secret messages by using a special code stick called a scytale.

Here's how to do it:

1. Wind a strip of leather around a stick.
2. Write a message on it.
3. Unwind the strip and send it to its destination.
4. The receiver winds the strip around his stick—and reads the message.

The First Codebreaker

One of the first people to break a code was an Arab called Abu Yusuf al-Kindi (c. A.D. 801–873), who created a brilliant and simple method of **deciphering** codes. Some letters are used more often than others. The most common are "e" and "t." First you look for the most common letter in the message, and change it to "e." Then change the second most common letter to "t." Soon you start to build up the uncoded words. This method is called "**frequency analysis**."

Abu Yusuf al-Kindi was a man of extraordinary learning. Among his many interests were astronomy, mathematics, medicine, science, and music.

The Polybius Square was invented more than 2,000 years ago by the Ancient Greek historian Polybius (c.203-120 B.C.).

How to send messages in the dark using the Polybius Square

1. Hold two flashlights, one in each hand.
2. Find the first letter of the message on the square. You can pinpoint it using the vertical and horizontal rows of numbers (so A is 1-1, L is 3-1 and so on).
3. Use the flashlights to flash the numbers. For H, flash the right-hand flashlight twice, then the left-hand flashlight three times. 2-3 means H.
4. Use this method to signal each letter of the message.

	1	2	3	4	5
1	A	B	C	D	E
2	F	G	H	I/J	K
3	L	M	N	O	P
4	Q	R	S	T	U
5	V	W	X	Y	Z

Top Secret

Ciphers Get Tougher

Once people knew about frequency analysis, it became much easier to break a cipher. Now spies and codemakers had to invent more difficult ways of hiding words. Italian Leon Battista Alberti (1404–72) made the first great breakthrough in modern ciphers more than 500 years ago. He used not just one but two alphabets to hide messages—one for the odd letters A, C, E and so on, and the other for the even letters B, D, F, etc. He also invented the first cipher disc. This was a simple tool for turning messages into code. The disc had two rotating rings of letters, one for original text, and the other for the cipher letters.

Leon Alberti was an architect, mathematician, artist, and writer.

Alberti invented a simple type of cipher disk around 1467. The inner and outer rings can be rotated to change the cipher.

CIPHERS AND PLOTTERS

During the 1500s, several new codes were developed. Some were almost impossible to break, but others were much simpler.

An Unbreakable Code

In the 1550s, a clever new cipher appeared. It was called the Vigenère Cipher after Frenchman Blaise de Vigenère (1523–96), one of its inventors. The cipher set out the alphabet 26 times in rows. The first letter of a message could be **encrypted** from Row 1, the second from Row 10, and so on. But how did the person receiving the message know which row was being used? Both sender and receiver had to know the key word. So if the keyword was CODE, the first letter would come from Row 3 (which starts with C), the second from Row 15 (which starts with O), the third from Row 4 (D), and the fourth from Row 5 (E). With this keyword, SPY becomes UDB in code.

Vigenère's "square" used 26 alphabets. Each alphabet starts one letter after the line above it.

Queen of Plots

In 1586, Englishman Anthony Babington planned an uprising to overthrow Queen Elizabeth I. The new ruler would be her cousin, Mary, Queen of Scots. Mary was held prisoner and closely guarded, but Babington was able to smuggle coded messages to and from her hidden in empty beer barrels. Elizabeth's agents soon **intercepted** the messages. They found the cipher was an easy one to break. The messages proved that Mary was involved in the plot, and she and all the plotters were executed.

SPY FILE

Gilbert Gifford
(1560–90)

Gifford was a double agent. He worked for Elizabeth's spymaster Sir Francis Walsingham, but joined Babington's plot under cover. Babington grew to trust Gifford and gave him the task of delivering the coded messages to Mary —hidden in the stopper of a beer barrel.

This coded letter was written by Mary, Queen of Scots. Queen Elizabeth I's agents intercepted Mary's letters and deciphered them.

The Great Cipher

In the late seventeenth century, a father and son set out to create an unbreakable code. Antoine and Bonaventure Rossignol worked for King Louis XIV of France. Their "Great Cipher" was used for most of King Louis' official records. Within a century the secret of the system was forgotten, and no one could read the records. It was not until 1893 that an expert French analyst managed to crack the Great Cipher.

Who was the Man in the Iron Mask? The answer was only discovered when the Great Cipher was broken in 1893.

Top Secret

One of Louis XIV's letters contained a big secret, which was only revealed when the Great Cipher was broken. The letter contained the real identity of the mysterious Man in the Iron Mask, a long-term prisoner once believed to be the King's twin brother. The mystery was solved when the Great Cipher was broken in 1893. A decoded royal letter said the masked man was a disgraced general.

Charles Babbage began designing the first ever computer in the 1820s, but it was not built until 1991.

Numbers for Sounds

How did the Great Cipher work? The Rossignols decided to replace **syllables** with numbers. A syllable is a unit that makes up a word—the word SYLLABLE itself has three syllables (sil / lab / bul). In the Great Cipher, each syllable was replaced by a number. No wonder it was almost impossible to **decipher**! For example, sil would be one number, *lab* a second number, and *bul* a third number.

Charles Babbage
(1791–1871)

Babbage was a brilliant British mathematician who made the first **programmable computer**. In 1854, he was challenged to be the first person to break the Vigenère Cipher. He succeeded—and the British army used the cipher during the Crimean War, which began that year.

13

MIGHTY MACHINES

Spies sent their secrets by hand until the invention of the **telegraph** in 1833. After this, and the invention of the **radio** in 1894, sending codes would never be the same again.

Messages by Air

Messages now could be sent and received in seconds. To do this, new systems were developed—such has the dots and dashes of the **Morse Code**, or speaking hidden messages over a radio. But both systems had a big disadvantage— enemy spies could easily pick up electronic messages. The messages would still have to be put into code.

The dots and dashes of Morse Code messages were sent electronically, then printed out on a long strip of paper.

Sir James Alfred Ewing
(1855-1935)

Scottish engineer Ewing loved solving crossword puzzles. He also taught courses in magnetism and electricity. In 1914, at the outbreak of World War I, he was appointed manager of Room 40. This was the British codebreaking headquarters in the Admiralty Building in London. Ewing employed other crossword experts to help decode intercepted German naval messages.

SPY FILE

Cutting the Cable

One of the first things the British Army did at the beginning of World War I was destroy the German communications system. A ship tore up the undersea cables that carried messages between Germany and the U.S. This meant the Germans had no safe way of sending information to the U.S. They could send **telegrams** through other countries, such as Sweden, or they could use the radio. Both of these methods could easily be picked up by Allied agents.

Top Secret

The Zigzag Cipher is a simple way to disguise words.

1. Draw three lines, one above the other.
2. The message is WAR IS DECLARED. Write the letters in a zigzag on the lines, like this:

```
W     S     L     D
  A I D C A E
    R   R   R
```

3. Now you have three new words, in code:
   WSLD AIDCAE RER

The Zimmermann Telegram

Throughout most of World War I, the U.S. government refused to take part. But all that changed in 1917. British codebreakers in Room 40 of the Admiralty Building in London picked up a telegram from German minister Arthur Zimmermann to his ambassador in the United States. It said that Germany planned to help Mexico attack the United States. The British showed the message to U.S. president Woodrow Wilson, who immediately declared war on Germany. The United State's entry on the Allied side helped to end the war more quickly.

Arthur Zimmermann sent his famous 1917 telegram in a cipher which changed letters into groups of numbers. British experts in Room 40 of the Admiralty Building in London were able to break most of the cipher in a single day.

The Codebreaker Who Saved Paris

In March 1918, the German army was close to defeat. It launched a last desperate attack in Northern France, which pushed the **Allies** back. Soon the Germans were close to Paris. The Allies had to find out the location of the final attack. But the Germans were sending messages in a code called ADFGX, which seemed unbreakable. Frenchman Georges Painvin worked for the next three months to crack the code. Finally, exhausted and half-starved, he deciphered enough to learn the German plans. Paris was saved.

Georges Painvin worked tirelessly to break the German code. He did so just in time to stop a crucial enemy attack near Paris.

SPY FILE

Joseph Mauborgne
(1881–1971)

In 1917, U.S. Army officer Mauborgne helped make a vital change to the Vigenère Cipher (see page 10). His idea was to use a **random** keyword made up of letters chosen by chance instead of a normal one, so the keyword could be "ltsugh!" This really confused the enemy! The random keyword was changed after a message was **encrypted**.

PURPLE AND ENIGMA CIPHER MACHINES

The world of codes is a battle between the makers and the breakers. By the end of World War I, the code breakers were on top. But when World War II broke out, new cipher machines soon changed that.

A Machine of 26 Million

One of the most famous cipher machines was the Enigma. It was created by the Germans and used by German spies to send messages during World War II. Enigma had a keyboard like a typewriter, but inside was a series of rotating discs, each displaying an alphabet. When a letter key was pressed, the discs turned varying amounts, thus changing the letter pressed. This system could produce an amazing 26 million different combinations of letters, making it very hard to break.

Members of the German Luftwaffe (air force) use an Enigma cipher machine. One airman types in the letters of a message, while another records the enciphered or deciphered letters.

Cracking the Code

The mysteries of Enigma quickly began to be solved by the Allies. By 1939, agents in Poland made the first breakthrough in understanding many German coded messages. They passed this vital information to the codebreakers in Britain who used it to crack the Enigma cipher in 1941.

SPY FILE

Alan Turing
(1912–54)

Turing was a brilliant mathematician. He was head of the team at Bletchley Park who were trying to break enemy codes during World War II. He designed an early form of computer called a "bombe." This could store all the possible letter combinations that could be made by Enigma. The computer was then used to decipher the Enigma messages.

The Enigma cipher machine used by Germany in World War II.

Bletchley Park in England was the headquarters of the Allied codebreakers during World War II. Their success remained top secret until long after the war was over.

Breaking Purple

Meanwhile, in the Pacific, U.S. forces were fighting against Japan. The Japanese also had a cipher machine, known as Purple. They believed no one would be able to decode messages sent through Purple. But U.S. and British intelligence teams had broken the code by 1940. They had even built replica Purple machines —without ever seeing one.

"PURPLE"

THIS IS THE LARGEST OF THREE SURVIVING PIECES OF THE FAMOUS JAPANESE DIPLOMATIC CIPHER MACHINE. IT WAS RECOVERED FROM THE WRECKAGE OF THE JAPANESE EMBASSY IN BERLIN, 1945.

PURPLE

The Purple cipher machine was similar to, but not the same as, Enigma. Purple could also produce 26 million combinations of letters.

Top Secret

In 1940, U.S. codebreaker Francis Raven made a major breakthrough in understanding the Purple machine:

1. The Japanese divided each month into 3 periods of 10 days.

2. On the first day of each period, they changed the key to the cipher.

3. Therefore, the key remained the same for another 9 days. This made interception work much easier for U.S. Intelligence.

Early Warnings

The Japanese never guessed the Allies were reading their messages. A lot of valuable information slipped through. In 1942, the Americans suspected a big Japanese naval attack in the Pacific. Some believed it would target Hawaii. But Purple messages said that the fleet was heading for Midway Island north of Hawaii. U.S. planes and warships were waiting when the Japanese arrived, and they won a major battle.

The breaking of the Purple cipher enabled the U.S. Navy to defeat the Japanese in the Pacific.

THE CODE TALKERS

Even the cleverest codes are usually broken in the end. But there is one type of disguise the enemy would never understand—a foreign language that only a few people can speak.

The Perfect Secret

During World War I, the U.S. Army used several Native American speakers to send and receive radio messages. These included the Comanche, Cherokee, and Choctaw peoples. Hardly anyone outside the tribes could understand them. The Germans soon realized what was happening and during the 1930s Hitler sent secret agents to the U.S. to learn these languages. But one proved too difficult for them—Navajo.

SPY FILE

Samuel Tom Holiday (born 1924)

Holiday was brought up on a Navajo **reservation** in the U.S. At 18, he joined the U.S. Army and trained to use the Navajo code. He was often in action behind Japanese lines, sending messages about enemy troop positions. Holiday was awarded the U.S. Congressional Silver Medal in 2000.

Hiding Words

In World War II, the Pacific islands were the scene of terrible battles between Allied and Japanese forces. U.S. troops found that cipher machines were too slow and big to use during the hand-to-hand fighting. The radio and telephone were much quicker and easier. However, vocal messages were not safe because they were uncoded, and many Japanese understood English. The Americans had to find a way of hiding spoken words.

Top Secret

The Comanche had no code word for Hitler in their language. Instead they called him "crazy white man."

A U.S. radio communications center operating on a "duck" (an amphibious military vehicle) in the Philippines during World War II. U.S. soldiers found it hard to keep radio messages in English secret, because the Japanese could easily intercept them and interpret them.

Unknown Navajo

Again the Native American language Navajo seemed perfectly suited for the job. In 1939, there were fewer than 30 non-Navajos in the world who could speak it, and none of them were Japanese. More so, it was very difficult, and almost no Navajo had ever been written down. The U.S. Army gave a test to two Navajo radio operators. They were able to encrypt, send, receive, and translate a message in just 20 seconds. The cipher machine took 30 minutes!

Navajo soldiers send coded messages using a portable radio during fighting in the Pacific in World War II.

Navajo words used to describe aircraft and ships:

Aircraft carrier:	TSIDI-MOFFA-YE-HI	(bird carrier)
Dive bomber:	GINI	(chicken hawk)
Destroyer:	CA-LO	(shark)
Fighter plane:	DAH-HE-TI-HI	(hummingbird)
Submarine:	BESH-LO	(iron fish)

Top Secret

Into Battle

More than 400 Navajo people were trained as code operators during World War II. Each one had to learn a special Navajo alphabet, as well as a list of Navajo codewords for military objects and place names. Most were sent to the Pacific, where their work played a big part in the Allied victories. The Japanese failed to crack the mystery code.

This book listed the Navajo alphabet and hundreds of Navajo code words.

Philip Johnston
(1892-1978)

Johnston was brought up on a Navajo reservation where he learned the language as a child. In 1942, he suggested to the U.S. Army that they use Navajo for their codes and helped set up the training. He also took part in writing the Navajo dictionary.

USING CODES TODAY

Modern computers have made huge changes to the making and breaking of codes and ciphers. These are now harder than ever before. But are they any better?

Spy satellites intercept radio messages and send them to tracking stations on the ground.

Faster and Better

Modern computers work much faster than the old cipher machines and can create new codes very quickly. They are also used to help break codes. Several computers linked together have an almost unlimited speed, and can be used to test every single letter or number combination on a cipher.

Computers today can make and break codes at high speed.

Keywords

Even with computers, modern codes have become much more difficult to break. One of the biggest problems in the past was that both sender and receiver had to know the keyword to be able to make the code work. In the past, keywords were often written in codebooks, which could be stolen or leaked to the enemy. These were called **private keys**. Today, most codes have two keys: one is kept secret, while the other isn't. Anyone can make a code and send a message with the public key, but only someone with the secret key can decipher it.

SPY FILE

Martin E. Hellman
(born 1945)

Professor Hellman is not a spy, but he helps to make and break codes. He helped invent the public keyword system in 1976. This technology is used in many different ways today. For example, when you pay for something over the internet, you are using Hellman's public keyword system, which ensures the safe transfer of money.

Top Secret

Modern military radio systems can encrypt a voice message and then send it—in complete silence. Only someone on their own side with special equipment can receive it and work out what the message is. Enemy agents cannot hear any sound at all.

How to Stay Secret

One fact is certain about codes: they are all unsafe. Modern spies know they can never trust a code or cipher completely —sooner or later the enemy will crack it. Spies today stick to simple rules to keep their codes working as long as possible.

- Change codes often. Alter the settings and keys for cipher machines to keep the other side guessing.

- Use a private unwritten code, known only by the sender and receiver. This can include nonsense words which mean something special to you, but nothing to a stranger.

Modern **phone scramblers** are hard to spot. This person seems to be using an ordinary cell phone. But is he?

- The best code is one nobody suspects you're using. It can be disguised inside everyday conversation. For example, you can use a cell phone which is easy to trace, but talk about ordinary things like football, cars, and films which have a coded meaning.

- Break the message into several parts and send them separately. Use different ways of sending the code—e-mail, letter, telephone call, text. Terrorist groups such as al-Qaeda use several couriers to carry parts of a message, so none of them knows the full meaning.

SPY FILE

Jonathan Jay Pollard (born 1954) American double agent Pollard spicd for Israel in the U.S. His greatest success was to pass on a photocopy of the 10-volume manual giving codes and details of the U.S.'s global surveillance network. Pollard was captured and imprisoned in 1986.

Modern detector machines can spot even the tiniest marks on a sheet of paper.

GLOSSARY

Allies a group of nations, including Britain, Russia, and the United States, who were united against the "Axis" nations, led by Germany, in World War II

cipher a system of secret writing where letters are rearranged or replaced to hide the meaning

cryptograph a device for deciphering coded messages

decode to convert a message from coded text into plain text

decipher to change a coded message into the plain, or original, text

encrypt to change a message into code using a cipher

frequency analysis a way of trying to break a cipher. Codebreakers look for the letters or numbers that occur most often in a message, then they try replacing them with the most frequently occurring letters in normal texts

intercept to stop or interrupt a message on its way to its intended recipient

mole an agent of a foreign power who works within a government organization and secretly sends out information

Morse Code a code where each letter of the alphabet has its own pattern of long and short signals (dots or dashes). The code was invented in the United States by Samuel Morse, and was used to send and receive messages during several wars

phone scrambler   an electronic device that "scrambles," or jumbles up, telephone signals so that unwanted listeners cannot hear them

private key   the code key used by the person who receives an encrypted message through the public key system. Only the receiver knows this key

programmable computer   a computer that can be fitted with a program (set of instructions) that performs certain tasks with numbers or letters

radio   a device for sending messages through the air using electromagnetic waves

random   without a pattern

reservation   an area of land set aside for Native Americans

syllables   a unit of sound in a word. For example, the word cottage contains two syllables: cott / age

telegraph   a system for sending messages in Morse Code, using long or short electronic pulses

telegram   a message sent by telegraph and written or printed on paper for delivery

INDEX

WEB FINDER

www.nsa.gov/kids/home_html.cfm
Crypto Kids™ web site. Provides fun cryptology games and facts.

www.history.navy.mil/faqs/faq61-4.htm
The Navajo Code Talkers' dictionary. Teach yourself the uncrackable code.

www.bletchleypark.org.uk/
The British national codes and cipher center website. Take a virtual tour of Britain's wartime codebreaking headquarters.